All About Animals
Polar Bears

By Christina Wilsdon

Reader's Digest Young Families

Contents

Chapter 1
A Polar Bear Story

Wild Words

A male bear is called a **boar**. A female bear is called a **sow**. A baby bear is called a **cub**.

The female polar bear stretched her legs and yawned. She was eager to leave her den in the snow. She had been inside it since October. Now it was March—six months later! Mama Bear could not wait to go outside.

But Mama Bear had not just been napping in the den all winter. She had also given birth to two babies. That was why she had dug the den in the first place.

Mama Bear's two little cubs were born in December. Each one weighed a little more than a pound. They were covered with a thin fuzz instead of fur and could not see or hear. Mama Bear cuddled them close as they drank her rich milk.

Now the babies were busy, furry cubs that could see and hear. Each one weighed almost 30 pounds—about as much as a human two-year-old. Like Mama Bear, the cubs were also ready to leave the warm, cozy den.

Mama Bear squirmed through the den's tunnel first. She sniffed the air for danger. Then she moved aside to let Baby Bear and his sister come out.

Ice Bears

The Inuit people of northern Canada call the polar bear *nanuk*, which means "ice bear."

At first, Baby Bear was afraid. He pressed close to Mama Bear. So did his sister. The air felt cold and nipped at his ears. Bright light dazzled his eyes.

Mama Bear's stomach rumbled. She had not eaten since October. She had lived off the fat in her body for all these months. But her fat supply was almost all gone now. She was ready to travel to the coast, where she could hunt for seals.

But Baby Bear and his sister could not make this trip yet. They needed more time to get used to being outdoors in the cold. They also needed more time to exercise and strengthen their leg muscles.

So Mama Bear and her babies stayed close to the den for a few weeks. Baby Bear romped and wrestled with his sister. The three bears slept in hollows scraped out of the snow. They went back into the den only when there was a big storm.

Dig It!

A female polar bear digs her den in a heap of snow. The den usually faces south, toward the sun, to add a bit of extra warmth. The body heat of Mama Bear and her cubs also warms up the den.

Den Mothers

Female polar bears that are going to have babies are the only polar bears that spend the winter in dens. The other polar bears continue to roam and hunt.

Biggest Bears

Polar bears are the biggest bears in the world—bigger even than grizzlies!

What a Meal!

A polar bear can eat as much as 100 pounds of food at one time.

One day, Mama Bear turned to her cubs and made a deep coughing sound. It meant "Follow me!" Then she set out for the coast. Baby Bear and his sister stepped into the big paw prints she made. Sometimes, when the going was rough, they climbed onto Mama Bear's back, and she carried them through the snow.

Mama Bear had made this trip many times before. She knew that she would find seals along the coast. She knew the seals were giving birth to their pups in snow dens on the ice. She would show her cubs how to find these dens and catch the seals inside.

The cubs watched Mama Bear hunt. But they also found lots of time to play. The two cubs chased each other through the snow. They made holes in the ice by smashing it with their front paws. If they went too far, Mama Bear made a moaning noise to call them back.

When it was time for the cubs to drink some milk, Mama Bear dug a hole in the snow, then sat in it as if it were an armchair. Baby Bear and his sister snuggled close to her.

Baby Bear and his sister will soon start eating meat. They will stop drinking milk. But they will not leave Mama Bear. They will stay with her for another two years, learning how to be a grown-up polar bear.

Chapter 2
The Body of a Polar Bear

Polar bears are the world's biggest meat-eating land animals!

Super Size

Polar bears live in one of Earth's most severe habitats—the Arctic. The Arctic is a place of ice and snow at Earth's northern end. In winter, temperatures drop far below freezing. Cold winds and snowstorms sweep the land. Trees cannot grow in the frozen soil. These treeless plains are called tundra.

Polar bears have changed, or adapted, over thousands of years to Arctic life. One adaptation is size. Big bodies lose heat more slowly than small bodies—and polar bears are huge! A male polar bear can weigh from 770 pounds to 1,500 pounds. At 1,500 pounds, he would be about half the weight of a midsize car!

When standing on all fours, a male polar bear is only about 4 feet high, but he's 10 feet tall when he stands on his hind legs. A bear this tall would have to duck to go through a doorway without hitting his head! Females are about half the size of males.

Wedge Shape

A polar bear's body is shaped differently than the bodies of other bears. A polar bear's head is longer and more pointed. Its neck is longer, too. This gives the bear a shape like a wedge. Being wedge-shaped helps a polar bear zoom through water when it swims.

A Furry Snowsuit

A polar bear is completely covered with fur except for its nose, lips, eyes, and the black pads on the bottom of its paws.

The color of a polar bear's fur helps it blend in with its environment of snow and ice. The outer fur is made up of long, hollow hairs called guard hairs. Although they look white, guard hairs have no color—they are clear. Like snow, guard hairs look white because they reflect sunlight. But at sunrise and sunset, a polar bear may look pink or orange—or blue on a foggy day!

Guard hairs also help waterproof a bear. They are smooth, so water slides off them. This helps stop water from seeping into the fur and reaching the skin.

Color Changes

Over time, a polar bear's fur sometimes turns yellow or brown. This is caused by eating a lot of seal fat and by the sun's rays.

Under the guard hairs is a fuzzy layer of fur that helps hold warm air close to the bear's body. The skin itself is black. This dark skin soaks up heat and light better than pale skin would. The black skin shows through on hairless parts of the bear, such as its nose and lips.

A layer of fat lies under the skin. A well-fed bear may have a fat layer that is 5 inches thick to help keep it warm on land and in icy water.

A polar bear is so warm inside its "snowsuit" that it sometimes rolls in the snow to cool off!

Full of Fur

Just one square inch of a polar bear's skin can contain more than 9,000 hairs!

This is one square inch.

The fur on the bottom of a polar bear's paws stops the bear from sliding on ice and snow. The black pads are rough with tiny bumps that add extra gripping power.

Bigfoot Bears

A polar bear has gigantic feet. Each paw can be 12 inches wide! A polar bear could hide a foot-long ruler just by planting a paw on it.

Big feet are a useful adaptation to life in a land of snow and ice. They work like built-in snowshoes, spreading out the bear's weight so that it does not sink into snow or crash through ice. A polar bear may also shimmy across thin ice on its belly or on its elbows and knees to spread out its weight even more.

Having large paws also helps a polar bear swim. Its front paws are partly webbed between the toes. The webbing helps the paws work like flippers when the polar bear dog-paddles in the water. The big back paws are used for steering.

Paws and Claws

Each polar bear paw is tipped with five long, hooked claws. The claws help polar bears grip the ice. This is especially useful when the polar bear climbs out of the water onto ice.

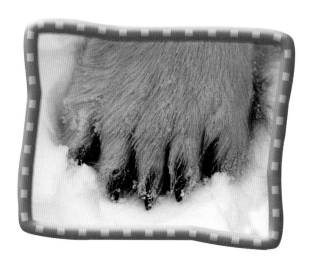

Chapter 3
Polar Bears on the Prowl

Polar bears are very patient. They sometimes wait for long hours at a seal's breathing hole for the seal to stick its head out.

Waiting for a Meal

The polar bear is a predator—an animal that eats other animals to survive. Its main prey is the ringed seal, but a polar bear will also eat other types of seals.

Ringed seals live throughout the Arctic Ocean. They spend lots of time underwater, but they must come up to breathe. So a ringed seal makes holes in the ice that covers the water. These holes are called breathing holes. A seal pops its head out of a breathing hole to get fresh air. It also enters and exits the water through these holes.

Polar bears know that if they sit and wait by a hole, a seal may pop up. This kind of hunting is called still-hunting.

A polar bear that is still-hunting first finds a hole. It can even sniff out a breathing hole that has been covered by a pile of snow.

Then the bear settles down by the hole to wait. It may sit down or lie on its belly, with its chin resting on the ice. Then it stays perfectly still. It doesn't move a muscle until a seal pokes its head out of the hole. Only then does the bear lunge! It grabs the seal by the head and drags it onto the ice.

Hunting for a Meal

Heaps of snow often drift over breathing holes. In spring, ringed seals carve dens into these drifts. Their pups rest inside these dens. A polar bear that is still-hunting can smell and hear a pup inside a den. Quietly, the bear stands up on its hind legs. Then it smashes open the den with its front paws.

A polar bear also hunts by sneaking up on seals that are lying on the ice. The bear lowers its head, then slowly creeps toward the seal. When it gets very close, the polar bear charges at its prey. Sometimes the seal is able to escape by diving through a breathing hole and disappearing.

A polar bear also sneaks up on resting seals by swimming. The bear paddles quietly up to the edge of the ice. Then it bursts out of the water to grab a seal by surprise.

Sea Bears

Polar bears are very much at home in the sea. In summer, they sometimes spend hours in the water just for fun! They can stay underwater for 2 minutes at a time and swim up to 40 miles without stopping to rest!

Blubber Bears

Polar bears are the only bears that have blubber, a thick layer of fat under the skin. Blubber helps keep them warm in the Arctic's icy water and frigid air.

Polar bears use their superb sense of smell to find seals and other food.

A polar bear eats only the skin and fat of the seals it catches, which means there's lots left over for other creatures.

Polar Bear Meals

Polar bears depend on seals for most of their food, but they also eat other animals. Big polar bears prey on adult walruses. Smaller polar bears go after walrus pups. Polar bears sometimes catch white whales called belugas. This happens when belugas get trapped in a small patch of water surrounded by ice. The bears grab the whales and pull them out of the water.

Polar bears also eat fish, seabirds and their eggs, and any leftovers they find. They will travel for miles to feed on a dead whale lying on shore.

Other animals feed on the polar bears' leftovers—and there is plenty left over, because a polar bear does not eat every bit of the seals it catches. It eats only the seals' fat and skin. It does not usually eat the meat. A polar bear needs lots of water to digest meat, but it can't drink salty seawater to get the water it needs. A polar bear would have to eat snow to get enough fresh water— and this would make it very cold!

Leftover Luck

Arctic foxes closely follow polar bears. They eat any scraps that polar bears leave behind. Gulls and ravens also feed on polar bear meals. Young polar bears eat leftovers from the meals of older bears.

Arctic Fox

Chapter 4
Polar Bears Together

Playtime for male polar bears sometimes means a wrestling match in which they try to knock down the other bear!

King of the Chill

Polar bears are loners. They do not live in groups. They do not seek out other bears for company. But sometimes even polar bears must spend time with other bears.

Sometimes polar bears see one another when they are hunting for food in the same area. They may seem to form a group if many polar bears come to one place to feed at the same time, but they are not together.

Male polar bears may ignore each other when they meet. But sometimes the two bears play. They stand on their hind legs, shove each other, and try to knock the other one down. Scientists have watched bears play for nearly an hour in this way. The bears do not hurt each other in these fights.

But their play-fighting is also practice for real battles. These battles take place during the mating season, which runs from April to May. Male bears fight fiercely over females during this time. They scratch and bite each other, sometimes leaving scars on their opponent's head and neck. Some males have so many scars from battles in their lives that they look like they have stripes.

Polar Places

A territory is a place that provides an animal with both a home and food. An animal considers its territory to be its own and will fight to defend it — even against animals of its own kind. Brown bears and black bears each have territories, but polar bears do not. They just head for places where there are lots of seals.

Bear Pairs

A male polar bear uses his sense of smell to find a female bear. He tracks her down, sometimes for miles. A scientist once tracked a male polar bear that walked 60 miles while on the trail of a female bear!

A female bear with cubs will not let a male bear near her. Male bears sometimes hurt or kill cubs. A female will attack a male to drive him away even before he comes close to her family.

But a female bear without cubs is ready to mate again in spring. Male bears for miles around know this, because as many as six will arrive in her neighborhood at about the same time. They growl at each other and sometimes fight.

Finally, one male succeeds in chasing away the others. The female polar bear lets the winning male bear come near her. They spend a few days together. Then they part company, each going back to live on its own.

When a Polar Bear Meets a Grizzly...

Polar bears and brown bears (grizzlies) sometimes mate. A cub that is half polar bear and half brown bear is often white when it is born. It may grow up to be brownish gray, pale yellow, or even white with brown patches!

A male and female polar bear nuzzle and sniff one another only after the male has chased away any competitors.

Polar bear cubs take naps
just as human kids do.

Care Bears

The strongest bond between polar bears is between female bears and their cubs.

Female polar bears are devoted moms. They watch their cubs carefully and warn them away from danger. They chase away male bears that might hurt the cubs. If cubs misbehave, their mother nips them or presses them against the ground.

Cubs spend their first year following close behind their mother. They watch her closely and copy what she does. This is how they learn to hunt. Sometimes cubs get bored sitting quietly. They start playing and spoil their mother's still-hunting!

But cubs learn their hunting lessons well over time. A one-year-old cub can catch a seal pup by itself. A two-year-old cub wanders away from its mother's side and can catch bigger seals.

Most cubs stay with their mothers for two and a half years. They are big enough to take care of themselves by then. Cubs in one part of Canada spend just one and a half years with their mothers. Scientists are studying these bears to find out why.

Chapter 5
Polar Bears in the World

Lands of Ice and Snow

Polar bears live where it is cold most of the year and the ocean is covered with large sheets of ice, called floes. In fall, polar bears move from land to floes that form near shores. They look for seals in big cracks in the floes and for seals' breathing holes.

In spring, sea ice melts in southern parts of the polar bears' world. The bears travel farther north to find ice that is still solid.

In some places, all the sea ice melts, and polar bears must stay on land until the water freezes again.

Where Polar Bears Live

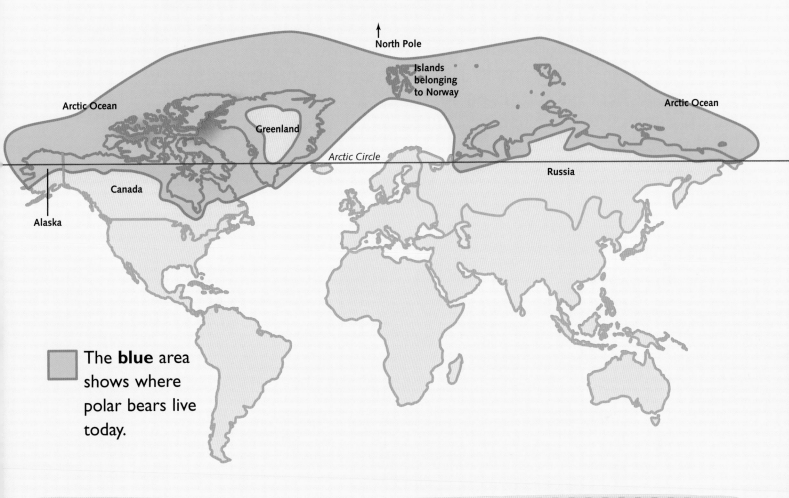

North Pole

Islands belonging to Norway

Arctic Ocean

Greenland

Arctic Ocean

Arctic Circle

Russia

Canada

Alaska

The **blue** area shows where polar bears live today.

Polar bears live mainly in the Arctic. The Arctic lies above a line marked on maps that is called the Arctic Circle. Trees do not grow above this line.

Polar bears live along Arctic coastlines in Canada, Russia, Greenland, and islands belonging to Norway. They also live in the United States, in Alaska.

The Future of Polar Bears

The polar bear's only predators are humans. Nations with polar bears signed The International Agreement on the Conservation of Polar Bears in 1973 to control hunting and to protect polar bear habitat. Even so, the biggest threat to polar bears is damage to their habitat caused by oil spills, pollution, and global warming.

Scientists have found that ice is melting sooner in spring and forming later in fall in Canada, where many polar bears live. This means the bears have a shorter season for hunting seals, their main food. Less time often means less food.

Scientists have also found that sea ice is shrinking in other parts of the Arctic. Polar bears now have to swim much farther to reach ice. Some bears cannot make it, and they drown.

Many people are working to find ways to slow global warming. They hope that polar bears will benefit from their work.

Fast Facts About Polar Bears

Scientific name	Ursus maritimus
Class	Mammals
Order	Carnivora
Size	Females up to 8 feet long
Weight	Males to 1,500 pounds Females to 880 pounds
Life span	15-18 years in the wild 30 years in captivity
Habitat	Arctic tundra and pack ice
Top speed	25 miles per hour

Save Energy, Save the Polar Bear

You can help preserve polar bears and their Arctic habitat by saving energy in your home. Here are four easy ways:

- Put on a sweater instead of turning up the heat.
- Turn off your TV and computer when you're not using them.
- Recycle cans, bottles, paper, and other items.
- Take a quick shower instead of a bath.

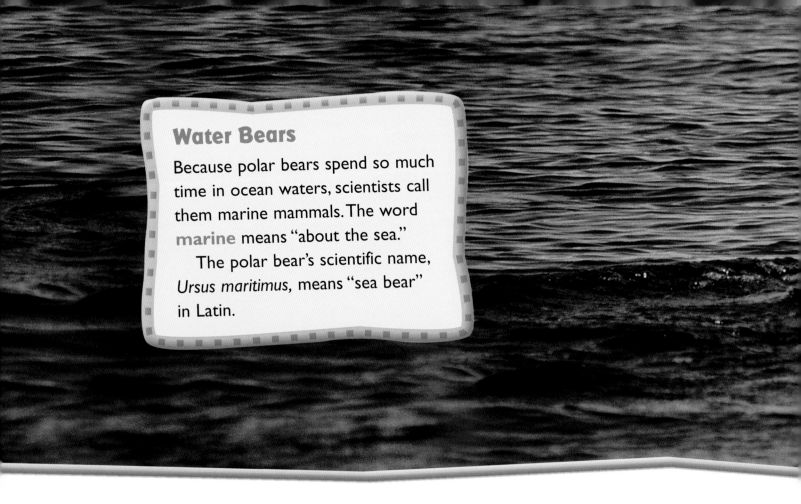

Water Bears

Because polar bears spend so much time in ocean waters, scientists call them marine mammals. The word **marine** means "about the sea."

The polar bear's scientific name, *Ursus maritimus,* means "sea bear" in Latin.

Glossary of Wild Words

adaptation a change over time in an animal's body or behavior that helps it survive in its habitat

arctic northern lands and oceans where it is cold and snowy much of the year

blubber a thick layer of fat under the skin that helps keep an animal warm

boar a male bear

breathing hole a hole that a seal digs in the ice to use as an entrance and exit as well as for coming up for air

conservation the protection and preservation of land, animals, plants, and other natural resources

cub a baby bear

floes sheets of ice on the ocean

global warming an increase in the average temperature of the Earth that causes a change in climate

guard hairs long hairs that form the outer layer of a polar bear's fur

habitat the natural enviornment where an animal or plant lives

predator an animal that hunts and eats other animals to survive

prey animals that are eaten by other animals

sow a female bear

species a group of living things that are the same in many ways

still-hunting a way of hunting that involves sitting still and waiting by a seal's breathing hole

tundra a big area of land in the Arctic region with no trees and a permanently frozen layer of soil

wedge something that is thicker at one end and thinner at the other

Index